HEADstart

WHALES & DOLPHINS

The Oceans' Largest Creatures Explained in Glorious Colour

MAUREEN HILL

C̶E

CAXTON EDITIONS

HEADstart

WHALES & DOLPHINS

First published in Great Britain by
CAXTON EDITIONS
an imprint of
The Caxton Book Company,
16 Connaught Street,
Marble Arch, London, W2 2AF.

ISBN 1 84067 020 7

A copy of the CIP data for this book is available from the British Library upon request.

With grateful thanks to Helen Courtney

Created and produced for Caxton Editions by
FLAME TREE PUBLISHING
a part of The Foundry Creative Media Company Ltd,
Crabtree Hall, Crabtree Lane,
Fulham, London, SW6 6TY.

Printed and bound in Singapore

Contents

Introduction

Whales, dolphins and porpoises are very closely related to each other. They have the family name of 'cetacea'. The word cetacea comes from a Latin word 'cetus' meaning 'a large sea animal' and a Greek word 'ketos', a 'sea monster'. Although they live their entire lives in the water they breathe air and give birth to baby versions of themselves rather than eggs. These animals are not fish, they are 'mammals' – warm-blooded creatures, like human beings.

There is a great deal that we do not know about these creatures. Human beings have only just begun to investigate their life cycle, social groups, behaviour, where they live, and how they communicate. In fact, scientists believe there may even be types of whale, dolphin or porpoise that we do not know about.

It is thought that whales, dolphins and porpoises developed from a four-legged land mammal about 60 million years ago.

These creatures have been important to humans for thousands of years. There are many stories and legends that have built up around dolphins, porpoises and especially whales. There is a story in the Bible about a sailor called Jonah who was swallowed by a whale and lived in its stomach until the whale spat him out.

Although not all scientists agree, many people believe that whales, dolphins and porpoises are very intelligent animals.

In the past, whales, dolphins and porpoises have been hunted by humans. They were hunted for their skin, their bones, their meat and for the oil that their bodies produce.

Whales

We usually think of whales as being huge creatures. Many of them are very large indeed. Some types, or 'species' of whale can be over 30 metres long. But not all whales are the same and the smallest whales are about the size of a dolphin, at two to three metres long.

They are well adapted to living in water. They move through the sea by propelling themselves with their large tail fin, shaped rather like the wing of an aeroplane. They use the fins on the side of their bodies to steer.

One of the main problems of living in water is keeping warm. Mammals are warm-blooded creatures, unlike fish. To keep them warm at sea whales have a thick layer of fatty tissue underneath their skin which insulates them. This is called 'blubber'.

Some whales are able to remain under water for an hour or more and can dive to depths of over 1000 metres. They have a specially adapted breathing system which helps them do this. Whales breathe in before diving, but instead of storing oxygen in their lungs they store it in their muscles and blood. This is where the oxygen is most needed. On very long or deep dives some whales can cut off the supply of blood to the parts of their body where it is not needed.

When a whale surfaces after a dive it breathes out and releases a fountain of liquid from the top of its head. This is called the 'blow'. Each species of whale has its own type of blow but all are thought to include condensed water vapour, some sea water and perhaps tiny droplets of oil or fat. The blow comes out of a single blowhole in some whales and a double blowhole in others.

Different Species of Whale

There are basically two types of whale – the 'toothed' whales and the 'baleen' whales. Within each of these two basic types there are a number of different species.

The toothed whales have teeth and they feed on fish and squid. Baleen whales tend to be larger and do not have any teeth. Instead, they have a baleen plate that acts like a sieve. Baleen is a horny substance that is arranged in strands rather like a brush. Baleen whales scoop up huge mouthfuls of water in which there are small sea creatures such as krill and tiny fish. The throats of baleen whales often have pleats on them that allow the mouth to expand. The water filters out of the mouth, leaving the food behind.

Beluga whales are toothed whales. They are unlike most other whales because they are white. They are generally found in the shallow waters of the Arctic where their colouring acts as camouflage against the Arctic coastlines and icebergs.

Another whale of the Arctic is the Narwhal. It is also a toothed whale and it has one very long tusk. The legend of the unicorn is thought to have grown from sightings of Narwhals. Very occasionally a Narwhal will grow two tusks.

Beaked whales are a group of toothed whales that have a beak-like mouth. The Bottlenose whales are also included in this group. Hardly anything is known about these whales. They live far out at sea and scientists have few opportunities to study them.

The Minke whale is the smallest of the baleen whales with a length of 7–10 metres. The Blue whale is the largest, and most baleen whales are between 10 and 20 metres long.

Blue Whale

The Blue whale is the largest creature on earth
and probably the largest mammal that
has ever lived. The female Blue whale
is slightly larger than the male and
has been known to reach a
length of 31 metres and to
weigh between 100 and 120
tonnes. Females have been recorded as weighing
as much as 200 tonnes at the end of the feeding season.

Blue whales travel between the warmer seas near the equator
and the cold seas of the polar regions. The whales mate in
the warm seas during the winter.
Feeding is done in the colder
waters of the Arctic

or
Antarctic
during the
summer months.
The whales follow the line
of the retreating icecaps. Their
favourite food is krill.

Most whale species carry their babies for about a year. The Blue whale's pregnancy is about 11 months long. The mother returns to the warmer, temperate seas to give birth to the baby during the winter months. Baby whales, called calves, are fed milk from their mothers for about six months before they start feeding on an adult diet. In some species of whale the calves may be fed by their mothers for about three years.

Unlike most whales, Blue whales are not very sociable. They are usually seen alone. Sometimes they can be spotted in pairs, although this is often a mother and calf. Even when Blue whales are feeding in large numbers there seems to be no sense of community or communication between them.

Whale Groups

Baleen whales such as the Fin, Humpback, Right and Bowhead whales are sometimes seen together in groups. However, these groups do not seem to stay together for more than a few hours. It is thought that baleen whales need a much wider area in which to search for food and so cannot be as physically close as toothed whales.

Toothed whales seem to be far more sociable. They travel in groups called 'pods'. These pods can vary in size from three or four to hundreds of whales. Some pods contain different species of whale. Sperm whales form groups of young adult males, groups of mature males and groups of mixed young whales called 'nursery' pods.

There are also groups of females with calves and one adult male.

Many studies have been made of the Orca, also known as the Killer whale. We have learned that they are very sociable

animals. They live in pods of between three and 25 members. The membership of a pod is stable; the whales stay together for several years. In some pods one Orca will catch the prey and share it with the others. Sometimes, several pods will join together to form a 'superpod'.

Orcas show much of their social behaviour above water. They have been observed slapping their tails on the surface and popping their heads above the water. They also can be seen 'breaching', leaping completely out of the water.

Whale Song

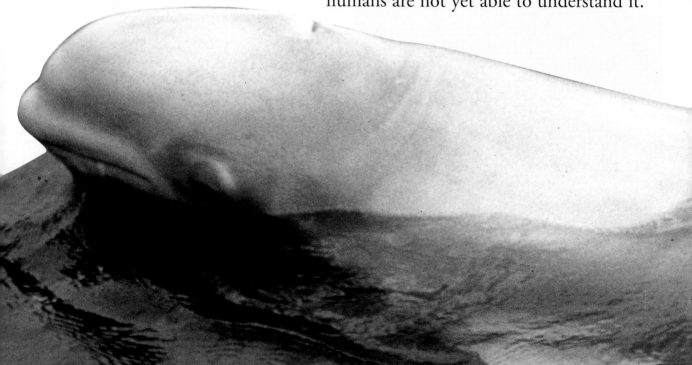

Whales make sounds. For hundreds of years sailors have heard the sound of whales at sea. The Beluga whale was given the nickname the 'sea canary' by sailors. However, we are unsure exactly how these sounds are produced. It is thought that the sound is not produced through the mouth as it is in humans. Instead, the sounds come through either the gap in the whale's nose or through the 'melon' which is located in the forehead.

The sounds that whales produce are very varied. Whistles, groans, screams, moans and clicks are all sounds made by whales. Some of the deeper sounds can be heard hundreds of miles away. The different sounds have different uses. Clicking sounds are produced to help the whale navigate, through a system called 'echolocation'. Other sounds are used to communicate with other whales. It is sometimes said that whales have a language, but humans are not yet able to understand it.

Scientists have been recording whale sounds for a number of years. One of the most fascinating of whale sounds is the song of the Humpback whale. It is thought that these songs are mating calls. The songs are rather like human songs in that the whales use repeated sounds and phrases. A single song can last from six to 35 minutes. Usually the song is repeated, sometimes for several hours. Within a certain area the song is the same, although each individual whale has its own recognizable 'voice', or way of singing.

Strandings

Occasionally, a whale or group of whales can become stranded upon the shore. Sometimes they are already dead when they are washed ashore. In this case the whale has died at sea, probably of natural causes, and currents have carried the body on to the beach.

However, sometimes the whales are still alive when they are washed up on to the shore. If this happens it is important to return them to the sea as quickly as possible. Although whales can breathe on land they can overheat very quickly. The blubber that protects them from the cold water also heats them up if they are out of water for too long. The whales must be kept cool by spraying them with water or covering them with wet cloths while attempts are made to get them back to sea, though rescuers must make sure that the blowhole is left uncovered and free from water.

When groups of whales are stranded rescuers sometimes find that if a single whale is returned to sea it will re-strand itself in order to be with the rest of its group.

A number of reasons for 'stranding' have been suggested. Some people believe that the whales come too close to the shore by accident, while trying to escape from the noise of shipping, earthquakes or storms. It may be that in shallow waters the whales' echolocation systems break down and they lose their way or get separated from their group. Some stranded whales have been found to have tiny parasites in their inner ears, which might also confuse their sense of direction.

Recently it has been suggested that some whales, like birds and insects, can navigate by using the earth's magnetic field, in much the same way as humans navigate by using a compass. Many strandings occur where the magnetic fields cross, confusing the whales.

Hunting

For hundreds of years humans have hunted whales. For a long time the hunters only took a small number of whales. The skin, meat, oil, even the bones of the whales would be shared among the community to help it survive. But as time went on humans became greedy and began taking more and more whales from the sea so they could sell the valuable oil and meat.

Throughout the eighteenth and nineteenth centuries there was huge demand for whale oil, used in oil-burning lamps, and baleen, known as 'whalebone', which was used to make ladies' corsets. Many of the slower moving species of whale became extinct or were hunted until only a few remained. Then the development of faster steam-powered boats, and a harpoon shot from a cannon, enabled the whalers to hunt the faster species of whale, such as the Blue, Fin and Sei whales.

Some whales even take their names from their usefulness to whalers. The Right whale was so called because it was the right whale to hunt. It lived close to the

shore, moved very slowly and floated when it was dead. All of this helped the early whalers, who were in small boats, using hand-held harpoons. It was also a right whale because it was rich in oil.

The Sperm whale is named after the milky-white oil it produces, rather like the fluid in which sperm is carried. This oil is of very high quality and was much sought-after in the past.

In the twentieth century people began to realize that the hunting could not continue. Many species of whale were close to extinction. In 1982 a 'moratorium', a total ban, was put on all commercial whaling. Although that ban is still in place, some countries continue to catch hundreds of whales each year claiming it to be scientific research. Some small communities, like the Inuit people are allowed to hunt a small number of whales each year, as they have done for hundreds of years, in order to help protect their way of life.

Marine Environment

The marine environment changes depending on the depth of the sea. The deepest parts of the oceans are deeper than the height of Mount Everest.

Scientists divide the ocean into four layers. The first layer covers the top 100 metres. This is where most sea creatures live and is where the light is strongest. Below this there is a layer known as the 'twilight zone' that reaches down to about 1000 metres. Below this are two further layers that are in constant

darkness. These dark layers are inhabited by strange fish and other creatures. Many of these creatures have never been seen by humans.

At all layers live microscopic plants, 'phyto-plankton', and microscopic creatures, 'zooplankton'. Fish, squid and shellfish eat the zoo-plankton. Toothed whales, dolphins and porpoises eat the fish, squid and shellfish. Baleen whales eat the zooplankton and fish.

Whales, dolphins and porpoises live and feed in the top two layers. Some whales can dive to depths of 1000 metres, the bottom limit of the twilight zone. Most dolphins and porpoises cannot dive deeper than 300 metres.

The continental shelf is a gentle slope for many miles out to sea. Once the slope reaches about 100 metres it then drops suddenly to the depths of the ocean.

Echolocation

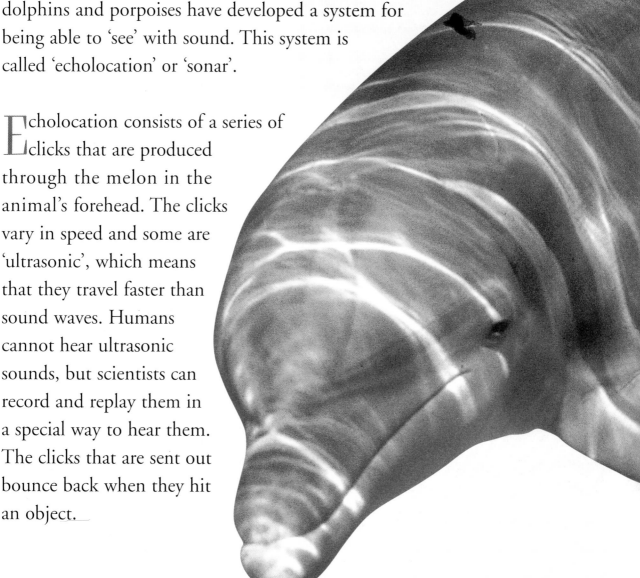

Whales, dolphins and porpoises have eyes that can see both in and out of the water. However, under the water their sense of hearing is much more useful as the light from the surface disappears as they dive deeper. Underwater, many whales and all dolphins and porpoises have developed a system for being able to 'see' with sound. This system is called 'echolocation' or 'sonar'.

Echolocation consists of a series of clicks that are produced through the melon in the animal's forehead. The clicks vary in speed and some are 'ultrasonic', which means that they travel faster than sound waves. Humans cannot hear ultrasonic sounds, but scientists can record and replay them in a special way to hear them. The clicks that are sent out bounce back when they hit an object.

Toothed whales use echolocation both for navigating their way through the water and for hunting. They are able to tell very precisely the size, shape, and their distance from an object just from the sounds that are bounced back to them. For instance, when hunting they can distinguish between a cod and a herring. Tests with toothed whales have shown that they can distinguish between two balls when a difference in size is so tiny the human eye would find it difficult.

Baleen whales do not seem to use echolocation but their sense of hearing is very important. They can tell which direction a sound comes from and, helped by the fact that sound travels faster and further underwater, they are able to hear over very long distances.

Dolphins and Porpoises

Dolphins and porpoises are very closely related to whales. They are often classed as toothed whales. Sometimes animals like the Orca and Pilot whales are classed as dolphins, but generally dolphins and porpoises are much smaller than whales.

Porpoises look different from dolphins in that they are slightly fatter (have a more rounded belly), with a blunt snout and flat, square teeth. Dolphins' snouts are more beak-like and they have conical-shaped teeth. There are only six types of porpoise, including the Common or Harbour porpoise and the Dall porpoise.

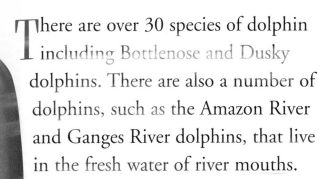

There are over 30 species of dolphin including Bottlenose and Dusky dolphins. There are also a number of dolphins, such as the Amazon River and Ganges River dolphins, that live in the fresh water of river mouths.

Dolphins and porpoises feed in the same way as toothed whales. They catch their prey, usually fish or squid, in their mouths. Their teeth help them hold the prey tightly but they cannot chew. Instead, they swallow the food whole, head first, to stop fish scales sticking in their throats.

They can travel very fast. Dolphins generally travel at about 30 kilometres per hour (km/h) but can go as fast as 40 km/h. Dolphins can dive to depths of about 300 metres.

Like several species of whale, dolphins and porpoises sometimes strand themselves on the shore, often in large numbers. When this happens it is important again to return them to the sea as quickly as possible.

Bottlenose Dolphin

Bottlenose dolphins are the most common species of dolphin. They can be seen in the Pacific, Atlantic and Indian oceans, as well as the Mediterranean Sea. They do not like the cold waters of the Arctic and Antarctic oceans. This is unusual, as most cetaceans prefer cooler seas.

They are very sociable creatures and live in groups, known as 'schools', of about 4–10 dolphins.

Sometimes these small schools join up with other schools, especially if they are hunting for food. A few dolphins are sent out to scout for a shoal of fish. They use echolocation to help them. When they find a shoal the dolphins line up and swim towards it, trying to push it into shallow water. Some dolphins leap and splash to scare the prey. Other dolphins circle around to trap the fish and then all the dolphins take what fish they want.

Bottlenose dolphins do not only hunt and feed together. They also play together. Bottlenose dolphins leap, turn somersaults and like to ride the waves. The dolphins also sleep close to one another. This gives them protection from attack by Orcas or sharks – the only predators they have to fear.

Bottlenose calves are born in late spring, after a pregnancy of about a year. The mother dolphin is usually helped in looking after the newly born calf by another female dolphin from the school. The mother dolphin will feed the calf for about a year.

Dolphin Talk

Most of the time dolphins produce noise. They produce clicking noises to help in echo-location. They also make whistling and squeaking noises to communi-cate with each other. Some scientists believe that the dolphins' squeaks and whistles are more like a language than simply signals of alarm or emotion such as anger.

In the last few years a large amount of work has been done in studying the noises dolphins make. Tapes of the dolphins' sounds are made using a 'hydrophone', a microphone for use under water. Many of the dolphins' sounds are within the human hearing range, so playing

them back is quite easy. What is difficult is decoding the sounds. Scientists are unsure whether the sounds stand for letters or words.

It seems that dolphins are able to have some sort of communication with humans. They can be taught to perform tricks or tasks. Some dolphins have been taught to make sounds that sound like human words. However, it is unclear whether the dolphins understand the idea of the word or just mimic it rather like a parrot.

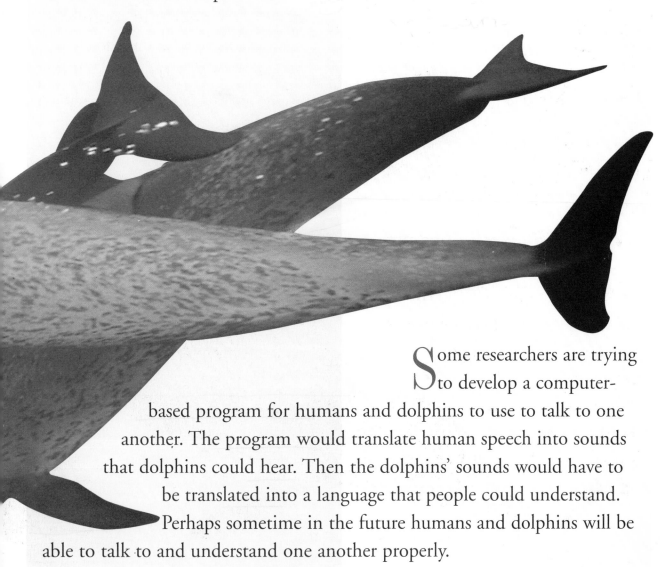

Some researchers are trying to develop a computer-based program for humans and dolphins to use to talk to one another. The program would translate human speech into sounds that dolphins could hear. Then the dolphins' sounds would have to be translated into a language that people could understand. Perhaps sometime in the future humans and dolphins will be able to talk to and understand one another properly.

Threats

Like whales, dolphins and porpoises were hunted and killed for profit by humans for many years. They were especially hunted for the oil in their blubber and in their heads. The oil was of a very fine quality and was used for the mechanisms inside watches. Oil from other sources is now used.

Porpoises and dolphins are not protected in the same way that whales are. Nowadays, there is little killing of these creatures for their oil, but fishermen still kill both dolphins and porpoises because they believe that they eat the fish that should make up their catches.

Throughout the 1960s and 1970s millions of dolphins and porpoises were killed by being accidentally caught in fishing nets. Fishermen would use huge

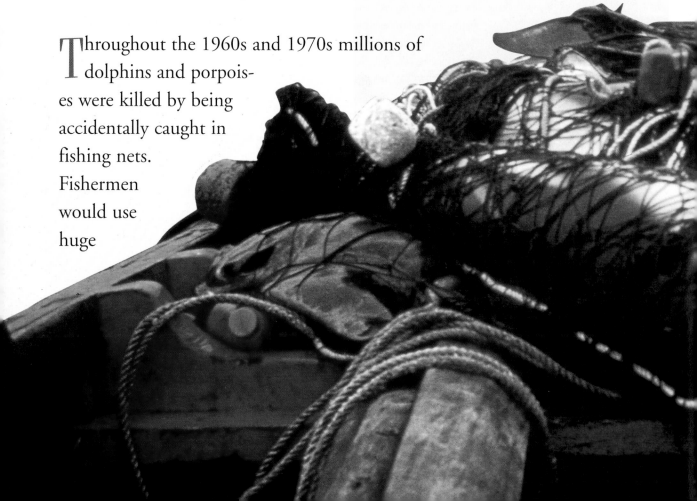

nets to catch tuna and the dolphins often became tangled up in them. Trapped under water in the net, the dolphins drowned as they could not reach the surface to breathe.

Campaigns during the 1980s, led mainly by people who refused to buy tuna, have meant that many fishermen have changed the way they fish. They use lines to catch tuna, or nets which are easier for dolphins to avoid or escape from. However, occasionally dolphins and porpoises still become trapped in fishing nets.

Dolphins and porpoises also face other dangers and difficulties through the activities of human beings. Occasionally, despite their echolocation systems, they can collide with boats. The noise and disturbance connected with busy shipping lanes or the offshore oil industry threatens their habitats. The over-fishing of many of the world's seas also means that there is often not enough fish for them to eat.

One of the most serious threats to dolphins, porpoises and also whales is pollution. These animals are at the top of the food chain in their environment. In the late 1980s hundreds of marine mammals including whales, dolphins and porpoises were washed up or found dead at sea. This happened all over the world, but particularly in areas like Europe and North America.

Investigations into this showed that the creatures had very high levels of dangerous chemicals, such as PCBs, inside them. PCBs are stored in fat and the blubber of marine mammals is all fat. Once inside the body PCBs make it difficult for the animal to resist disease.

The pollution gets into the animals' bodies by the simple process of the food chain. The chemicals and sewage that are dumped into the ocean are absorbed by microscopic marine plants. These are eaten by tiny marine creatures which are in turn eaten by shellfish and fish. The final predators in the chain are dolphins, porpoises and the toothed whales.

On Show

At one time it was possible to see dolphins, porpoises and some whales from the shore. They could be glimpsed at sea or in river estuaries. Nowadays, this is a rare sight in many parts of the world, mainly because the numbers of creatures have dropped so dramatically. The pollution in coastal and estuary waters also keeps away any sea life.

One of the most frequent ways in which people can see dolphins today, apart from on TV or film, is in aquariums. It is mainly the smaller toothed whales, porpoises and dolphins that are kept in aquariums. The large whales are simply too big to survive in the confined space.

Many people are beginning to question whether keeping such creatures in aquariums is a good thing to do. There is also concern

about whether it is right to use intelligent creatures to perform tricks, like jumping through hoops and begging for fish, for public entertainment.

Some people have been able to get even closer to dolphins with 'swim with the dolphins' programmes. Those who have done this say it is a wonderful experience, but some people are concerned that such close human/dolphin contact might transmit diseases between the species.

In some areas like the Californian coast, where whales come quite close to the shore, it is possible to join a boat trip to observe the whales. There are also similar schemes to enable observation of dolphins.

The Future

For hundreds of years cetaceans have been important to humans in a number of ways. There are many stories about dolphins rescuing humans from drowning at sea, or protecting them from shark attacks. The oil and meat they provide have also been used as a means of survival for some communities like the Aleut in Alaska and the Inuit who live in Greenland. This was acceptable when only small amounts were taken, but today, most people realize that several species have become extinct through large-scale hunting. They also realize something needs to be done to prevent some of the present species from becoming extinct.

The threat of extinction through hunting is beginning to lessen. The Pacific Gray

whale was given protection in 1946 and there are now about 24,000 of this type of whale. This is about as many as there were before commercial whaling began. However, it has taken 50 years for this species to recover. It is very important that the world-wide ban on whaling remains in place.

Although several countries have national laws against it, the hunting of dolphins and porpoises is not banned throughout the world, and countries such as Japan and Norway continually campaign for the hunting to start again.

For all cetaceans pollution from human beings' activities is the biggest problem. We need to stop dumping industrial and household waste into the seas and oceans, the animals' habitat. We also need to be very careful not to allow accidental pollution from the oil and nuclear power industries. It is very important that whales, dolphins and porpoises have some areas that are undisturbed; conservation areas at sea. We must also stop over-fishing which takes the food from the animals.

If we do not make changes in these areas it is very likely that several more species of cetacean will become extinct. As three quarters of our world is made up of seas and oceans the extinction of these creatures will be a bad sign for the future of humanity.

Places to Visit and Things to Do

The Whale and Dolphin Conservation Society – provides information about whales and dolphins throughout the world. You can adopt a dolphin – you give money to WDCS and they use it to support protection programmes in certain areas. You can choose one dolphin and they will give you information about it. The Whale and Dolphin Conservation Society, Alexandra House, James Street West, Bath, BA1 2BT. Telephone: 01225 334 511.

Natural History Museum – with a whole gallery given over to whales and dolphins including life-size models. The Natural History Museum, Cromwell Road, London, SW7 5BD. Telephone: 0171 938 9123.

Further Reading

Dolphins and Whales, Eyewitness Guide, Vassili Papastarrou, Dorling Kindersley.

Window of the World, Whales, Dolphins and Porpoises, Mark Carwardine, Dorling Kindersley.

Whales, Malcolm Penny, Puffin.

The Blue Whale, Melissa Kim, Riverswift London.

Whales and Dolphins, John Birdsall, Parragon.

In The Company of Whales, The Discovery Video Library Series

Web Sites

Smithsonian Institute Web Site – http://www.si.edu/resource/faq/start/htm for lots of information on Natural History including whales and dolphins. Smithsonian Institute, Jefferson Drive, South West 1000, Washington DC, USA. Telephone: 001 202 357 2700.

Greenpeace Web Site – http://www.greenpeace.org/ gives up to the minute information about all sorts of environmental issues, including activities concerning whales and dolphins. Greenpeace UK, Canonbury Villas, London N1 2PN. Telephone: 0171 865 8100.

Picture Credits

All photographs courtesy of Still Pictures.
Pages: 8, Christian Weiss; 9, Mark Carwardine; 10, H. Ausloos; 11, Christian Weiss; 12-13, Mark Carwardine; 13, C. Allan Morgan; 14, Steven Morello; 15, B & C Alexander; 16, Mark Carwardine; 17, Donald Tipton; 18, Mark Carwardine; 19, Christophe Guinet; 20-21, J.P. Sylvestre; 21, Mark Carwardine; 22, Roland Seitre; 23, Mark Carwardine; 26, Fred Bavenden; 28-29, Robert Henno; 30, Tom Walmsley; 32, Cyril Ruoso; 33, Kelvin Aitken; 34, Yigal-Unep; 38, S. Dawson; 39, Thomas Raupach; 40, Jeffrey Rotman; 41, Mark Carwardine; 43, Hellier Mason; 45, Jeffrey Rotman.